a letter to the prime minister

by ellyna merican

Koon Lifestyle
Petaling Jaya, Selangor, Malaysia.

www.koonlifestyle.com

Cover design and illustrations: Ellyna Merican

Limits of Liability/Disclaimer of Warranty:

Attention: Schools and Businesses

Koon Lifestyle books are available at quantity discounts with bulk purchases for educational, business or any sales promotional use.

For more information, email:
ellyna@koonlifestyle.com

for
mankind
as we hold hands
and tread this borrowed land.

i was scrolling through
my facebook feed
when i stumbled upon
a 3-minute 33-seconds video
that had changed my life forever.

it was a speech
by meghan markle
at a un women conference
on international women's day in 2015.

11-year old megan taught me
that every one of us
can become
the seed of change.

so one day,
i too decided
to write a letter
to my dearest
prime minister.

- the letter

contents

the beginning

i'm still dazed at this
coincidence of reality,
to be given the chance
to lead a nation twice
and become the oldest
state leader alive at 94
is definitely a rare feat
in this day and age.

- dear prime minister,

nonetheless,
i learned that our Creator
has a miraculous way
of piecing the puzzle
perfectly together.

voila!
everything that was
previously falling apart
now somehow falls
swiftly into place,
just like magic.

- the Creator's divine plan

deep down i believe that
He has brought you back
as our leader and put you
on a very critical mission –
to steer the entire *ummah* (mankind)
on the divinely-guided path.

- the chosen leader

something about
your leadership
deeply resonates
with my soul –
it's your care
and compassion
for the people.

in the year 1991,
you breathed
life into a vision
of an ideal malaysia,
the vision that could even
change the fate of the world.

as i'm writing this now,
it's already 18th of august 2019.
we haven't got much time left
to realize this vision.

- wawasan 2020 (vision 2020)

loss and chaos

there is an aching sore
in the pith of my heart,
as if a dagger had
pierced through it
a million times over,

as i begin to ponder
the fate of humanity
and every creature that
lives on, in and above
this earth and beyond.

oh how this heart
screams in agony!

- the heartache

nations are busy constructing
weapons of mass destruction,
spending lavishly on warfare
in the race for paper money,
fueled by the flames of greed
to prove superiority over others,

but it has caused us all a great divide
while the lives of innocent civilians
have perished in numbers far
too painful to even mention.

homicides and suicides
are common news today.

the act of corruption,
the act of destruction,
the act of killing,
the act of murder
have become the norm
for mankind,
destroying not just
our own kind
but even other
divine creations –
animals, plants,
oceans, rivers,
the land, sky
and beyond.

- flames of greed

thermometer readings
across the globe
steadily rise with
no signs of
cooling down
since the beginning of
the industrial revolution.

the past decade has been
the hottest years ever in history
since modern record-keeping
began some 140 years ago

and now we're all trapped
in our manmade furnace.

- the manmade furnace

the decayed remains of plants and
other organisms buried underneath
layers of sediment and rocks
have taken over 650 million years
to become the carbon-rich deposits
we know today as fossil fuels.

it is a fuel fashioned by nature –
under intense heat and pressure,
an energy source originating
in ancient photosynthesis.

world war 2 was a notable turning point
in history leading to our fossil fuel frenzy today –
the first war to be fought using aircraft and tanks,
the age of the modern vehicle came next,
followed by the electronics revolution.

- history of fossil fuels

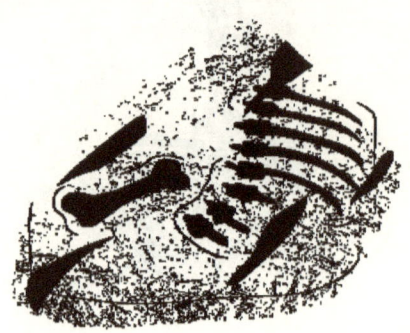

96% of the items we use each day require fossil fuels
to produce (and that's a modest estimation):

from the fuel for cars, trucks, ships, trains and planes
to the electricity that powers lighting, heating,
cooling, refrigeration and for operating appliances,
electronics and machinery

to our daily necessities – lipsticks, lotions, nail polish,
deodorants, shaving creams, shampoos, soaps,
toothbrushes, toothpaste, perfumes

to our daily fashion – clothes, shoes, bags, purses,
sunglasses

to common household items – curtains, carpets,
refrigerators, mops, dishes, detergents, dishwashers,
faucet washers, toilet seats

to construction – roofs, water pipes, rubber cement,
wire insulation

to automotive – car battery cases, car bodies, tires, oil
filters, fan belts

to healthcare – anaesthetics, vitamin capsules,
antiseptics, antihistamines, dentures

to entertainment – guitar strings, loudspeakers, paints,
paintbrushes, tennis rackets

to all the plastic bags we carry around with food and
things. they're the ones we stash our trash in, too.

- fossil fuels of today

combustion of fossil fuels releases
greenhouse gases that include carbon dioxide,
water vapour, methane and nitrous dioxide.

when sunlight reaches the earth
some energy is reflected back into space
and some is absorbed by the land and oceans
and is re-radiated into the atmosphere as heat.

but before the heat can make its way back
to outer space, these greenhouse gases
absorb and trap the heat in the atmosphere,
warming our planet even more than it should.

burning fossils fuels for energy has an
enormous toll on humanity and our planet –
from land, air and water pollution
to global warming,
to climate change,
to mass extinction.

- *carbon chaos*

it's worth underlining that
the fossil fuel and plastic
industries are closely linked
(since over 99% of the plastic we
choke every nook and cranny
of the earth is made from chemicals
sourced from fossil fuels).

just as we begin to understand
the dangers of plastic pollution
and take action to reduce our usage,
industry is poised to invest billions
to ramp-up plastic production,
incentivizing companies to manufacture
more and more plastic in the future.

with the production of plastic,
companies will surely find markets
to consume it (us, of course!),
thereby driving demand.

just as we keep burning fossil fuels
as fast as we can frack them,
we need to pause and ponder
over our current economic model
then question ourselves –
what happens when there
are no more fossil fuels left?

- the [no] future of fossil fuels

forests are more than just a sea of trees,
they are home to about 80% of the
planet's terrestrial biodiversity,
affecting almost every species on earth.

trees absorb rainfall and release
water vapour into the atmosphere.
in the amazon, over half the water
in the ecosystem is inside the plants.

tree roots anchor the soil,
reducing the pollution in water
by preventing polluted runoff.

without trees, the soil is free
to wash or blow away
which may lead to silt entering
lakes, streams and other water sources.
this greatly reduces local water quality
and results in poor health of populations.

it may also lead to vegetation growth problems
when cash crops like coffee, soy and palm oil
are planted, causing soil erosion because
their roots cannot hold onto the soil.

- *trees*

the role of forests in the water cycle
can be seen in real life:

dominican republic and haiti
may share the same island
but it seems like they are worlds apart.

while the former is regarded as a popular
tourist destination in the caribbean,
the latter is seen as one of the
world's poorest countries.

then we noted an interesting observation:

haiti has much less forest cover
in comparison to the dominican republic
and as a result, haiti has endured more
extreme soil erosion, flooding and
landslide problems as opposed
to its next-door neighbour.

- the role of forests in the water cycle

earth is home to about 3 trillion trees
but we lose 15 billion of them every year.

the world's plants and animals that
live in forests are losing
their habitats to deforestation.

deforestation is considered
the second-largest manmade source
of all greenhouse gas emissions
right behind fossil fuel combustion.

when forests are cleared to make way
for urbanisation, mining, logging
and agriculture, it releases nearly
a billion tons of carbon into the air yearly.

we're becoming more efficient at stripping
our forests than we are at replanting them.
now over 20% of our earth's greenhouse
gas emissions are caused by deforestation
as compared to 14% by transportation.

deforestation adversely impacts
medicinal research and threatens
the livelihood of populations who
depend on the animals and plants
in the forests for hunting and medicine.

- *deforestation*

at this very moment
the lungs of the earth
are drowning in flames!
forest fires are raging
in the heart of the largest
rainforest on the planet.

this time the wildfires
are so intense they're even
visible from outer space.

strong winds carry the smoke
from the blaze and envelope
nearby cities in a dark haze,
plunging brazil's largest city
into a night-like darkness
in the middle of the day.

wildfires often occur
in the dry season in brazil
but they are also deliberately
started to illegally deforest land
for cattle ranching and mining.

if the amazon touches
a point of no return,
the rainforest will turn
into a dry savannah
no longer habitable for
much of its wildlife and
instead of emitting oxygen,
it will start emitting carbon –
the major contributor
of climate change.

- our burning lungs

sometimes i wonder why
we don't hear news
of billionaires rushing in
with monetary aid
to save our rainforests
like they did when the
notre dame caught fire?

- dead silence

then it hit me hard
that these wildfires are
a human-made disaster
and since i identify as a human,
i've also become a contributor
to the destruction of the land and sea.

it's easy to point fingers
at others with our dirty hands
but it's tough to swallow our pride
and admit our own mistakes.

when you point
one finger at others,
there are three fingers
pointing back at you.

- the blame of shame

in my attempt to remedy this problem,
i begin to ask myself several questions
to arrive at the root cause:

do i use plastic? yes
do i fuel my car? yes
do i consume meat and poultry? yes
do i live in an urban area? yes
do i depend on fossil fuels?
you bet i do

and the list of questions went on…

is there anyone else
out there who is like me?
pretty much every
other urbanite, i guess.

a conclusion i can draw from this?
we are all equal contributors
to the destruction that spreads
like wildfire all over the earth today.

- the root cause

about 91% of the world's population
lives in locations where its air quality
surpasses the world health
organization's guideline limits,
typically in low- and
middle-income countries.

carbon dioxide, soot, smoke, mold, pollen
and methane are just some examples
of the common air pollutants responsible
for over 7 million deaths yearly.

air pollution leads to higher rates of
cancer, heart disease, stroke and
respiratory diseases such as asthma
from fumes of the ongoing combustion
of fossil fuels, land clearing and other
carbon-emitting human activities.

bad outdoor air caused approximately
4.2 million deaths worldwide
while indoor smoke is a constant
health hazard to over 3 billion people
who cook and heat their homes by
burning biomass, kerosene and coal.

while the link between dirty air
and physical health is much clearer,
the air pollution that triggers mental
health disorders in humans is much
less apparent but its effects
can be felt all around us.

air pollution is linked to increased
risks of depression, bipolar disorder,
schizophrenia and personality disorder.

for instance, children under 10 who breathe
polluted air are twice likely to develop
schizophrenia later in life.

it also causes less direct health effects
contributing to climate change in terms
of heat waves, extreme weather and
food supply disruptions.

[world health organization reports]

- air pollution and our health

approximately 30% to 40% of the carbon dioxide
from human activity does not stay in the air
but is absorbed by the oceans, rivers and lakes.

for decades, the earth's oceans have absorbed
massive quantities of carbon dioxide that
would have lingered in the atmosphere.

this prolongs the full impact of global warming
by significantly reducing the global temperature,
but for how much longer?

since humans are land mammals,
we're only able to see the effects of
climate change from the increased
carbon dioxide emission
into the atmosphere.

but when the impact of
climate change occurs underwater,
we humans are less likely to detect the problem
simply because the problem is not visible to us.

over the past 200 years, the ph level
of the ocean's surface has lowered by .1 units,
that's a 30% increase in acidity levels.
if this trend continues, the carbon dioxide
will become even more acidic.

marine wildlife is struggling to adapt to the
increased levels of acid in their habitat,
shells erode and species are forever poisoned.

- acidic waters

water is a peculiar yet
precious and finite resource.
all of the water on earth is alien
because it arrived on earth
from outer space – from ice
in meteors and comets.
our oceans formed
millions of years after
the earth took its shape.

every molecule of water on this earth,
inside us or any other living creature
has existed for billions of years,
endlessly cycling through rocks, air,
animals, plants and back again.
every molecule of water has gone on an
astronomical voyage before coming to us.

oddly, normal rules of chemistry
don't apply to water.
a water molecule is made
from two very light atoms:
hydrogen and oxygen.

given the earth's surface
temperatures and pressures,
water should exist
as a gas on earth and
unlike any other chemicals,
when water freezes it expands,
which is why ice floats on water.

overtime, this odd behaviour has
proven to be very beneficial –
by insulating the water underneath,
floating ice has permitted complex

life forms to survive and evolve on earth
despite the many ice ages that have
frozen the earth's surface solid.

water molecules can float upwards
against the force of gravity because they
love to stick to each other and can even
pull each other up through tiny channels,
like the blood vessels in our body that
supply oxygen and nutrients to our brain
and other parts of our body.

it's the same process that allows plants
to transport water from below the ground
to nourish the leaves and stems
that grow in the sunshine.

- wonders of water

today the physical, chemical and biological
properties of water have been altered,
making it unsafe for the ecosystem.

when contaminants such as
organic and inorganic materials, pathogens,
heavy metals and other toxins are present
in water, it instantly turns into wastewater.

- *wastewater*

ice is changing everywhere on earth.
massive ice fields, monstrous glaciers
and sea ice are disappearing, fast!

the poles of the earth are more sensitive
to any change in the earth's climate
than anywhere else on earth.
an increase in global temperature
caused by greenhouse gas emissions
over the past century has resulted in the
poles warming faster than lower latitudes.

this phenomenon is caused by the decrease
in the earth's albedo – whereby melting ice
uncovers darker land or ocean beneath
the earth, then absorbs more sunlight
instead of reflecting it back into space,
thus accelerating the warming and
melting of snow and sea ice.

billions of tonnes of ice in greenland are melting
50 years ahead of climate change schedules.

the famed snows of kilimanjaro
have melted more than 80% since 1912.

glaciers in the garhwal himalaya are retreating
so quickly that researchers predict the
disappearance of the most central and eastern
himalayan glaciers by 2035.

the formation of a lake high in the french alps
after a glacial snow meltdown in the intense
heatwave is an unusual and alarming sight.

- the big thaw

melting ice has increasingly stranded polar bears
on land leading to a "polar bear invasion" of a
military town on novaya zemlya, which is an
archipelago in the arctic ocean in northern russia.

you've probably seen images circulating online of
starving polar bears scavenging from dustbins for
leftover food and invading communities in
nearby towns and cities.

climate change has shrunk their natural habitat –
which is the ice they hunt on and these polar bears
have been shot dead when they came too close to
humans because we "fear" that they might
harm our lives.

- polar bear invasion

when temperature rises and ice melts,
more water flows from glaciers
and ice caps into the oceans.

ocean water warms and expands in volume,
resulting in a global sea-level rise.

however, the recent rate of global
sea-level rise has deviated
significantly from the average rate
of the past 2000 to 3000 years.

as permafrost soil thaws,
the collapse and erosion of coastline
and seafloor deposits may accelerate with
the arctic amplification of climate warming.

a sinking coastline and a rising sea level
combine to yield powerful
yet devastating effects.

- *sea-level rise*

every day we see
more and more wildlife
choking on the plastic
we dump into our oceans
in obscene proportions.

the ocean has become a
plastic-filled minefield
for numerous marine wildlife.

our social media newsfeed
is constantly bombarded with
appalling images and videos

of whales, dolphins and fish
that are washed ashore
with tonnes of plastic
jammed in their stomachs

while other marine wildlife
are caught dead in ghost nets
abandoned by fishermen.

- *the minefield of marine wildlife*

a cringe-inducing video that went viral
showed an olive ridley sea turtle
with a plastic straw up its nostril
and a team of scientists who spent
nearly 10 minutes pulling it out.

this video has somehow sparked
a global outrage which led to the
ban on single-use plastic in
many parts of the globe.

it became a foundation for
the zero-waste lifestyle movement
that is becoming more popular today
- a lifestyle that focuses on waste prevention
by redesigning resource life cycles
so that all products are reused
and disposed the most appropriately.

- the turtle and the straw

about 90% of all seabirds have
ingested pieces of plastic:

from bags to bottle caps
to synthetic clothing fibres.
what's even more tragic – they're even
feeding their young with it!

they don't just feed on plastic waste,
cigarette butts are even more common
on the beaches than straws or plastic bottles,
they're the most abundant type of ocean trash.

karen mason photographed an unsuspecting
black skimmer parent that mistakenly tries
to feed its baby a cigarette butt.

- when seabirds hunt for food

an indonesian woman
who purchased a mahi-mahi fish
from a market in the west java
made a terrifying discovery
when she found 8 plastic objects
inside the fish's stomach as
she was cleaning the fish
which was meant for cooking.

among the plastic items found:
an entire spoon,
a candy bar wrapper,
a deodoriser lid,
a lengthy strap of plastic
and other tiny plastic bits.

- what goes around comes around

animals everywhere on earth
are dying because of what
our hands have wrought,
we might as well call it
second-degree murder.

animals ingest so much trash that
there is little room left for food
because the trash blocks food
from travelling into their gut,
starving them to death.

other times sharp edges pierce
through their internal organs,
tragically killing them.

- second-degree murder

as we can clearly see,
all life forms within the ocean
play a vital role in maintaining
the marine food web.

dangers to the biodiversity in the ocean
not only affect the marine life food web
but it will eventually find its way
into the human food web,

especially with our heavy reliance
on fish and other seafood from the oceans
and clean drinking water from
springs, rivers, streams and glaciers.

- food web

waste is a common problem
in almost every country
but malaysia is officially ranked
as one of the world's worst when
it comes to plastic pollution.

as if dealing with our own waste
isn't enough, now there's the horror
of plastic waste being dumped
by other countries.

now we're walking down
the hall of infamy nicknamed
"the world's dumpster".

a staggering 19% of waste
clogs our drains, causing flash floods,
but an even larger portion of it
ends up in the ocean.

- *where the world sends its trash*

meet dennis.
a 24-year old
solo traveler
who took a trip to
the east coast islands
of *pulau kapas*
and *pulau perhentian*
in malaysia.

curious, i asked him to
observe the cleanliness of
our beaches and
share his experience,
but his response broke me:

"actually the plastic here
is already everywhere.
cannot even stand how
the people don't care for it at all.
it seems that nobody knows
that someday in the future
not big stone monuments
will be the last sign of humanity,
it will be beaches full of plastic ...sh*t."

- life in plastic

the fault is placed
firmly on human shoulders
as our relentless pursuit of a better life
has come at the expense of
mother nature's grief.

- that insolent drop of water

lo and behold!
soon a full force of
climate catastrophe
will plague our home
and it's going to get
much worse.

mother nature's
silent cries for help
have fallen on deaf ears
as we continue to
prioritise our selfish gains
with blatant disregard
for her well-being.

- her silent cries

a mass extinction
is already underway!

we're through only
the sixth mass extinction
since the last half-billion years,
yet we're on the path toward creating
a similar degree of carnage to that
wreaked upon the dinosaurs by
an actual asteroid that had hit
earth millions of years ago.

- *mass extinction*

the extinction
of the entire innocent species
is more than just a climate catastrophe
but it's a kind of cosmic sacrilege.

not only is it tragic, cruel and immoral
but absolutely blasphemous and
signals a direct revolt against God.

the Qur'an tells us that:

"the killing of an innocent soul is
comparable to the slaying of all mankind."

- cosmic sacrilege

in the publication
'the holy Qur'an and the environment',
there is a sentence that beautifully captures
the essence of every creation:

"for every species is not merely
an accidental feature of evolution
but a direct and blessed manifestation
of divine creativity."

the Qur'an also says:

"…every creature glorifies its Creator
but you understand not their praise."

- the divine creation

greta thunberg
is a swedish activist
who at the age of 15
began protesting outside
the swedish parliament in 2018.

her cause?
that immediate action be taken
to combat climate change.

her speech serves as
a rude awakening
to all of us earth-dwellers:

"around the year 2030,
10 years 252 days and 10 hours
away from now, we will be
in a position where we set off
an irreversible chain reaction
beyond human control,
that will most likely lead to
the end of our civilisation as we know it –
that is unless in that time, permanent
and unprecedented changes in all
aspects of society have taken place
including a reduction of
carbon dioxide emissions
by at least 50%."

given the chance to choose,
i'd rather listen to the
honest speech of a 15-year
young girl than the
biased news on media outlets
funded by ultra-wealthy,
profit-motivated parties.

her screams of terror
are the loudest to my ears
because our very future
is literally at stake here.

- *greta's warning*

the earth
is a container
of the living
and the dead.

there will be a day
where the sky brings forth
clouds of smoke that
envelop mankind
in a painful torment,

the day
the blast of the horn
will convulse all creations
except those He wills.
all the signs are clear
that the Hour is near.

we have been warned
of the day when man
will observe what his
hands have put forth.

- the Hour

the mirror

in the stillness of the night
off my mind wanders
beyond the earth's gates,

deep into the unknown,
searching for answers
to understand my big why.

i long for a temporary escape
from the noise and restlessness
of my daytime reality.

i find comfort and peace
when i craft stories in my head,
stories with happy endings.

- the spiritual voyage

as i drift further into dream state,
my imagination springs to life
and pulls me deeper.

like a child's curiosity
my spirit runs wild and free,

in gardens underneath
which rivers of white milk
and pure honey flow,

wearing garments of
fine silk and brocade.

- the dreamer

i needed a divine intervention –
the strength, courage and hope
to cure mankind's heart dis-ease
and heal my dying home,

so to my Lord i pray:

"expand for me my breast with
assurance and ease for me my task
and untie the knot from my tongue
that they understand my speech."

[Qur'an 20:25-28]

- a servant's prayer to the Lord

"Ta, Seen, Meem
these are the verses
of the clear Book."

[Qur'an 28:1-2]

Ta, Seen, Meem
H54 in base-19
6236 in base-10
the exact number
of verses in the Book.

if a single verse was added or removed
from anywhere in the entire Book,
this code would have been broken.

- the clear Book

and then i came across another
mind-blowing verse that translates to:

"there is not a creature (that lives) on the earth,
nor a being that flies on its wings,
but (forms part of) communities like you."

[Qur'an 6:38]

- communities

the night is celebrated
self-reflecting in solitude,

a mirror into my soul,

words are gracefully arranged
to serve as guidance.

- solitude

the sound of the drums
shake the lonely world,
a call to prayer echoes.

hymns of praise
break the silence,
intertwined by the
rooster's crows.

- at the break of dawn

a gust of wind
whispers in my ears,
calling my name
as if to summon
my heart and
all my senses.

it speaks to me
with words that are
softer than silk,

"be the seed of change"
it says.

- be

love and peace

i return from my spiritual
quest with a precious gem
in my heart – inner peace.

with an unwavering faith
i have found my big why –
it came in the form of a recipe
beautifully concocted by
dr patrick liew:

"the recipe to a life of
lasting joy and fulfillment
is a life of service
and a life of service
is a life of overflowing love.

there is a smallness to a life
lived in service to the self
whereas there is a grandness to a
life lived in service to others."

- a life of service

there is love in life.

love is a magical feeling
that sparks from within,
it creeps on you in silence
but you secretly crave its presence.

it sends shivers down your spine
and makes your heart dance
in a state of trance.

it's astronomical,
it's infinite,
it's inexplicable,

and it's best left
to the workshop
of your imagination.

- *love*

when you look into the universe
with your heart, you will see that
love is already out there
waiting for you.

all that is needed is for you
to use your senses to feel the love
and give love to the universe,

for the very source of love
comes from your own
beating heart.

- *self-love*

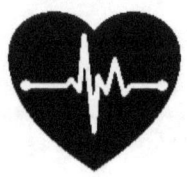

her love
transcends
beyond borders.

you were born
into this world
from her very womb.

the love you pour
into the relationship
with your mother

could win you
the golden ticket
to the highest of heavens.

- *a mother's love*

just like a woman's uterus
the soil is the womb
of mother earth,

a sacred home
that nourishes
the seed of life.

- *earth*

"indeed, in the creation of
the heavens and earth,
and the alternation of
the night and the day,
and the [great] ships
which sail through the sea
with that which benefits people,
and what God has sent down
from the heavens of rain,
giving life thereby to the earth
after its lifelessness and
dispersing therein every
[kind of] moving creature,
and [His] directing of the
winds and the clouds controlled
between the heaven and the earth
are signs for a people who use reason."

[Qur'an 2:164]

a parable of the present life –
it is like water that rains from the sky,
the plants of the earth absorb it
but then it becomes old plant,
dispersed by the wind.

- the drop of life

today, we have come to a one-time
"use it or lose it" moment on earth.

by 2030, we may hit the point of no return
where we can no longer keep global average
temperature rise to well below 2c.

the coming two to three years are a
critical window to execute bold
climate decisions that will determine
the eventual fate of humanity on earth,

whether we lock the world
onto a path to sustainable growth
or climate catastrophe by 2030.

- call to action

governments around the world are now
engaged in efforts to reduce greenhouse gas
emissions from fossil fuels to prevent
the worst effects of climate change.

at the global forefront, countries are committed
to reducing their carbon emissions with targets
as part of the 2015 paris agreement

while other entities including cities, states and
businesses have made their own commitments.

the paris agreement primarily focuses on
keeping the increase in global average
temperature to well below 2 °c.

- the world's pledge

under the paris agreement,
malaysia is committed to reducing
greenhouse gas emissions
by at least 45% by 2030
in relation to its 2005 gdp.

this target was set with:
"35% on an unconditional basis
and 10% on a conditional basis
upon receipt of climate finance funding,
technology transfer and capacity building
from developed nations."

malaysia is also committed
to maintaining at least 50% level of
forest and tree conservation.

the leading greenhouse gas
emission contributors in malaysia
comprise of the energy, transport,
manufacturing, industrial,
waste and agriculture sectors.

- malaysia's promise

the paris agreement
is just a paper-based promise,
the reality of the situation
is an entirely different story.

with the world's continuing reliance
on fossil fuels, many contend that
in addition to our efforts to replace
fossil fuels, it's also important to suck
carbon from the air by deploying
technologies such as carbon capture
where emissions are diverted
to underground storage or recycled
before they reach the atmosphere.

several commercial-scale projects globally
are already capturing carbon dioxide from
the smokestacks of fossil fuel-fired plants,
but its high costs do not permit
wider adoption of the technology.

advocates remain hopeful that
technological advancement
in the future will make it more
affordable for global-scale adoption.

- carbon capture

so i thought to myself,
hey, the process of carbon capture
seems somewhat familiar.

eureka! i actually learned this
in science class back in school.

the carbon capture mechanism
mimics photosynthesis – the process
used by plants and other organisms to
convert light energy into chemical energy.

this chemical energy is stored in
carbohydrate molecules such as
sugars which are synthesized from
carbon dioxide and water.

most of the water evaporates
back into the atmosphere
but a very small amount stays
inside the plant as sugar.

in most cases, oxygen is also released
as a waste product that is used to fuel
the organisms' activities.

- photosynthesis

so why not leverage on
mother nature's very own
carbon capture mechanism?

it's the cheapest option
to remove carbon
from the atmosphere
and combat a
catastrophic climate crisis.

it's a no-brainer!

there is no need
to rely on climate
finance funding or
technology transfer
and capacity building
from developed nations
to make a difference at home.

- nature's magic

i watched a short video on facebook,
part of a series called "what if".

a particular episode caught my attention –
what if we planted a trillion trees?

if we planted a trillion trees
we could offset a decade's worth of
our greenhouse gas emissions,
time we desperately need.

but to achieve this goal before 2030
will require a concerted
international effort.

a worldwide planting programme
could remove two-thirds of all
carbon dioxide emissions
in the atmosphere.

if every human on earth planted
just 150 trees, we could meet our
1 trillion tree goal quite easily,
but this is not very realistic.

so people have found solutions:

for example, tree planting drones
can plant up to 100,000 trees daily
which equals to about 50 veteran planters.

while many students take up
tree planting as a profitable summer job,
the more innovative of them have
found other ways to cash in.

whether we do it manually, by drones
or by robots, it's time to bring out
the big guns in this battle
to save our home planet.

by planting a trillion trees
half the battle is already won.

- what if we planted a trillion trees?

while the earth has lost half
of its trees since the last ice age
and planting a trillion trees
seems far ahead in our future,
it's certainly a mission that is
not impossible to accomplish.

despite the ticking time bomb
we're holding in our hands now,
there is still hope for humanity.

- hope for humanity

i recall the wise words of dr patrick liew
that made perfect sense to me
and connected all the dots.
he said:

"governments cannot solve key problems
of the world because politicians are
dependent on popular votes,
there are limitations to what they
can do and achieve.

universities and other educational institutions
cannot fully address these issues because
they are focused primarily on the
pursuit of knowledge.

charity bodies have been around for
thousands of years yet they cannot offer
a sustainable solution because they lack
systems, talents, finance, technology and
other resources to resolve these challenges.

we need a fourth key – every one of us.
when the people sector works closely
with the public and private sectors,
we can overcome these challenges."

- the fourth key

recently, the world is impressed by how
the philippines is tackling the climate change
issue by getting its people involved in the process.

it has passed a new bill that permits students
to graduate from schools and colleges only
after planting 10 trees each.

the philippines has been a strong advocate
in saving our planet, evident from its
impressive tree-planting initiative.
it has even broken a world record
for planting the most trees in an hour.

- tree planting project

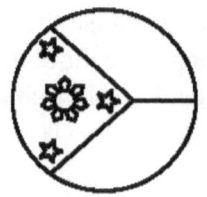

i read a beautiful story
about a couple who rebuilt
their deserted piece of land
of 600 hectares in aimores, brazil.

they planted more than 2 million
tree saplings in 2001
and 18 years later
their land now has
293 plant species,
172 bird species,
and 33 animal species,
some of which were
on the verge of extinction.

- if victory had a face

natural climate remedies
such as ending deforestation
and restoring degraded forests
on a global scale could potentially:

create 80 million jobs
and free 1 billion people
from the vicious circle of poverty

while contributing to a whopping
usd$ 2.3 trillion in productive growth.

- natural climate remedies

the "think global, act local" principle
is applied to organizations, businesses,
education and governance.

it urges employees, students and
citizens to consider the global impact
of their actions on the earth's health
and take action in their own
communities and cities.

individuals were coming together
to protect habitats and the living
organisms within them long
before governments started
enforcing environmental laws.

small steps in the right direction
will eventually result
in a quantum leap.

- think global, act local

a city that we should pay
close attention to is the
slovenian capital of ljubljana.
15 years ago, all its waste went
straight to landfill, just like ours.

but by 2025, at least 75% of
its rubbish will be recycled.
so how did this city do it?

this city realized how expensive
it was to have landfills that take up
space and discard useful resources.
so, it decided to change course:

in 2002, it started with separate
collection of paper, glass and
packaging in roadside container stands.

in 2006, the city began collecting
biodegradable waste door-to-door.

separate collection of biowaste will be
mandatory across europe in 2023,
but ljubljana was almost two decades
ahead of the curve.

in 2008, the city's recycling rate
was at 29.3%. it was still lagging
behind the rest of europe.

in 2013, every doorstep in the city
received bins for packaging and paper waste.
most controversially, scheduled collections
of the residual waste were cut by half,
forcing people to separate their waste

even more efficiently, which has led
to impressive outcomes.

today its recycling rate is 68% and
its landfill receives almost 80%
less rubbish, taking the top spot in the
recycling leaderboard of eu capitals.

this city now produces only 115 kg
of residual waste per capita annually
and even turns biowaste into
high-quality gardening compost.

the development of the most
modern biological waste treatment plant
in europe (rcero) has been a major contributor,
processing 95% of residual waste into
recyclable materials and solid fuel
and sends less than 5% to landfill.

however, a sustainable way ahead
is not just about processing waste,
it's much more important to
refuse, reduce, reuse and recycle.

on top of its door-to-door collection,
ljubljana has two household waste
recycling centers where citizens can
dispose their rubbish.

the one near rcero ljubljana is so popular –
it receives over 1,000 visitors daily
that the city plans to build at least
3 more with another 10 smaller
sites in high-density areas.

stuff that isn't broken gets reused.
items are checked, cleaned and
then sold at low prices by the facility.
it also organizes weekly workshops
that teach citizens how to fix broken things.

zero-waste stores are trending in ljubljana
and the voka snaga waste department
manages its own packaging-free
vending machines for household essentials.

since space is limited in the city centre,
voka snaga installed 67 units of containers
underground where the bins open with a
card issued to residents.

[the guardian reports]

- the green lifestyle

we embraced a beautiful concept
called "*gotong-royong*" in the past
which refers to communal work
in the malay and indonesian culture
by which members of a community gather to
mutually accomplish a task for special events
such as weddings or communal fundraising.

let's take a look at a typical
gotong-royong scene in the *kampung* (village)
when cooking for a wedding reception:

villagers who come to help out are assigned to
different tasks – some peel and chop veggies and
fruits, some take turns to stir cauldrons of a variety of
must-have dishes like *ayam masak merah* (chilli
chicken), beef korma, dhal gravy and *acar* (pickled
fruits and veggies) to accompany the signature
wedding menu, *nasi minyak* (spiced ghee rice).

a head chef conducts multiple taste tests
and seasons every dish to perfection
while others wash the dishes,
refill food and drinks and bus tables.

everyone gets their tasks done as they
chitter-chatter, exchange stories
and laugh together.

it's painful to note that *gotong-royong* is less
commonly practiced in today's more individualistic
cultures where there is less reliance on others
than in pre-industrial agricultural societies.

- *gotong-royong*

the *gotong-royong* spirit
must be rekindled
to strengthen the bond
of our local community
with a common goal:
to save our planet.

numerous fun activities
can be done together
as a community –

we can organise a
neighbourhood cleanup day
to pick up, sort and recycle trash
and clean our parks, lakes, beaches,
rivers and other public areas.

we can also kickstart
a green movement
to plant tree saplings and
build edible gardens
that will someday turn
into a sanctuary where
flora and fauna
can thrive again.

- community spirit

it took 96 weeks and
thousands of volunteers
to clean up versova beach
in mumbai, india.

the payoff?

hundreds of thousands of
sea turtle hatchlings
can be seen on the beach
for the first time in decades.

- the great beach cleanup

it's also a good idea to take a break
from our busy virtual lives once in a while
to reconnect with the earth's electrons.

this promotes intriguing physiological
changes and results in an improved
overall well-being.

according to total health:
"earthing (or grounding) refers to the act of
walking barefoot outside, or sitting, working,
or sleeping indoors, connected to conductive
systems that transfer the earth's electrons
from the ground into the body."

earthing offers remarkable benefits
that include better sleep and reduced pain.
it also stabilizes and harmonizes our
body's basic biological rhythms.

- earthing

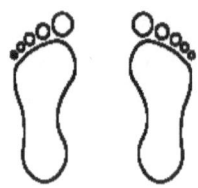

you love your house
to be clean, don't you?

you mop the floor,
vacuum the carpets,
dust the cabinets,
do the dishes,
wipe the windows,
and take out the trash.

you do it as often as
you can so it stays
neat and clean.

once upon a time
your mother's womb
was your home,

then you were born
into this world and
this body you're in
becomes your home,

you live on this earth
that houses you
and your home,

and when you die,
the earth that you
used to step on will
become your home.

- your home

before we enter 2020,
we must be fully equipped
to face the uncertainty and
complexities of the future
by incorporating nature's values
into our development plans
and demonstrating love
towards all creations.

taking action is the key
that unlocks the power
that we have in the form
of our free will – the ability
to choose and decide our fate
in this life and the eternal life.

even if the future seems bleak,
just keep holding on to faith
and remember that this world
is not the resting place,
but it is the testing place.

we must strive to
optimize this lifetime,
do our best in this test,
then leave the rest to
the Best of Planners,
our one and only Creator.

- your inaction is also an action

this worldly life is but
a ticking time bomb
anxiously awaiting doomsday –
the day the horn is blown.

- ticking time bomb

"verily
God does not change
the condition of a people
until they change
what is in themselves –
and that is their heart."

[Qur'an 13:11]

it all depends
on your intention –
if you intend to do good
and you perform good deeds,
goodness will unexpectedly
come pouring into your life.

- the heart

the ending

the Creator has crafted you from clay
and has perfected you in every way
and breathed into you of His *ruh* (spirit).

- how you came to be

"and to Him belongs
what is in the heavens
and what is on the earth
and what is between them
and what is under the soil

and if you speak aloud
then indeed He knows the secret
and what is even more hidden."

[Qur'an 20:6-7]

He is your Lord,
He is my Lord,
He is our Lord.

- the Lord of the worlds

there is one race
that we all belong
to on this earth –
the human race.

He created us
from male and female
and made us peoples and tribes

and He created the diversity of
our languages and our colors
that we may know one another.

- diversity

when we unite as one,
together we will rise
to our final abode
in the heavens above,

a location in the future of stars
where gravity goes so mad there
that space and time become
indistinguishable and the
structure of spacetime
becomes singular,

and to Him is due all praise
throughout the heavens
and the earth.

- unity towards singularity

you walk this earth not without purpose.
you have been bestowed with a divine task.
He has appointed you as a vicegerent on this earth.

He has put the land and sea under your control
and provided you with sustenance and
exalted you above many of His creations.

- the vicegerent

what good are your eyes
if you do not see?

what good are your ears
if you do not hear?

what good is your heart
if you do not feel?

- *senses*

remember,
your eyes speak
what your tongue hides.

- the naked truth

an urdu poet once wrote:

"every soul will taste death
but nobody knows of
his hour of death.

he may make plans
to live for a hundred years
but he never really knows
if he will live to see tomorrow!"

all he knows is that
every new day
is a day closer
to his death.

- death

when you depart
this dearly beloved world
and the veil that screens
your eyes is lifted,
many realities which
are hidden before
are now made
known to you.

- the final departure

if you are given
just one page
in a book,
the very last page
to write the ending
of your life,

how would
your story end?

- the last page

a letter to the prime minister
is a collection of prose
from the *a short piece* series
that takes a raw and in-the-moment look
at the dark reality of life today where
destruction on the land and sea
has appeared because of what
mankind's hands have wrought.

it takes readers on a spiritual voyage –
interweaving the nuances of life's
beauty and horror that eventually
transitions into a powerful
civilizational wake-up call
to fulfill mankind's duties
as vicegerents on earth.

- about the book

ellyna merican is an author of a collection of prose, *a letter to the prime minister*. her interest in writing sparked at the age of 3, inspired by her late grandfather, ba who first taught her her abcs and 123s. growing up, she dabbled in writing for fun, which has won her a few competitions in school, music festival tickets, beauty products and other freebies.

in 2017, after quitting her last 9 to 5 job as an events marketer, she kickstarted a globetrotting lifestyle that enabled her to explore exotic locales and understand different cultures. it was during her travels that she gradually found her voice and began to truly embrace her passion for writing, which gave her the ultimate freedom of expression.

she has ridden on the roller coaster of chaos to find her harmony and now pens her thoughts about spirituality and sustainability on her lifestyle blog, **koon lifestyle. koon** aims to serve as an edutainment platform that connects the community through short stories. she invites you to visit her website at www.koonlifestyle.com.

- about the author

www.ingramcontent.com/pod-product-compliance
Lightning Source LLC
Chambersburg PA
CBHW051355280526
45784CB00007B/2973

* 9 7 8 1 0 9 9 5 4 1 7 2 8 *